# Social
# Justice in
# a Changing
# World

# CONTENTS

## SUMMARY

1.  Welfare is now top of the political agenda. This publication, the second discussion document from the Commission on Social Justice, applies the values developed in our first report to the changing social, political and economic world. It starts from a simple proposition: that the policies and institutions designed to build the post-war peace fifty years ago are not adequate for the challenges of the 21st century.

2.  Britain's welfare state was the child of John Maynard Keynes' economic revolution and William Beveridge's social conscience. However, its fundamental assumptions - about full employment, the nuclear family, and the relationship of citizens to government - have been undermined by fifty years of history. There are new realities - a global economy based on skill and technology, family change based on the growing independence of women, political change based on new distributions of power - with which British public policy must come to terms.

3.  The fundamental insight of the Keynes/Beveridge welfare state - that wealth and welfare go hand in hand - remains true today. Wealth pays for welfare, and social welfare should promote wealth creation. Social and economic policy depend on each other. To be an effective Commission on Social Justice, we must equally be a Commission on Economic Opportunity.

4.  In our first publication, we defined social justice according to four key ideas: the foundation of a free society in the equal worth of all citizens; the right of citizenship that all citizens be able to meet their basic needs; the requirement that we extend to all citizens the fullest possible range of opportunities and life-chances; and the need to reduce and as far as possible eliminate unjust inequalities. In this publication, we set four objectives for public policy:

### The Objective of Security

Security comes from the prevention of poverty; relieving poverty is a second best.

### The Objective of Opportunity

What government can do *for* people is limited; but there are no limits to what people can be enabled to achieve for themselves.

### The Objective of Democracy

The more decisions that are made by the people, the better those decisions will be.

### The Objective of Fairness

Not all inequalities are unjust, but unfair inequalities should be reduced and if possible eliminated.

5.    The challenge for the Commission is to achieve these objectives in a rapidly changing economic, social and political world. Social injustice in Britain today is shocking, but its roots go back well before the election of Mrs Thatcher in 1979. The industrialised world must today come to terms with three great revolutions:

#### The Economic Revolution
- a revolution of skill, technology and work.

#### The Social Revolution
- a revolution of women's life-chances.

#### The Political Revolution
- a demand for a new relationship between
citizens and their government.

6.  There are two economic futures for Britain. The low road promises low wages and low investment, high unemployment, and conflict over a shrinking national product. The high road is one of high investment and high return, where we compete in the market for quality goods and services by combining Savile Row service, Marks and Spencer quality and C&A prices.

7.  The social revolution of women's life-chances demands action from government, including a fundamental review of social security, child care and social service provision. It also demands action from employers so that men and women can balance family and work commitments. And it requires changes within families, as relationships between women and men are renegotiated.

8.  The political revolution is not a demand for less government, nor more government, but better government. Distrust of the political class is based on the growing distance between the debates of elected politicians and the everyday concerns of the people they represent. Participation and not paternalism needs to be the basis of a new relationship between those who govern and those who are governed.

9.  The collapse of the conventional ideologies makes this a time of great political openness - a time to 'make the future'. That demands radical thinking. We suggest ten propositions about the strategies needed to advance social justice and economic opportunity in Britain. In brief, they are that:

    ●   Social justice is about more than poverty - it concerns us all.

    ●   Paid work for a fair wage is the most secure and sustainable route to financial independence; a modern form of full employment is central to social justice and economic efficiency.

    ●   The tax system should help us fulfil our obligations to each other, as well as insure ourselves. Redistribution of income is a means and not an end; social justice demands revenue to meet basic needs and extend opportunities, but there are limits of principle and practice on levels of taxation.

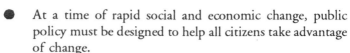

- At a time of rapid social and economic change, public policy must be designed to help all citizens take advantage of change.

- Social justice demands a widening of access to wealth.

- The British economy requires a major shift from short term consumption towards long term investment in people, ideas and infrastructure.

- A strong community must support its families; we cannot expect families to shore up weak communities.

- Social cohesion has an economic value in itself, and strong communities are the bedrock of economic regeneration.

- Citizens' rights should be strengthened, and matched by new responsibilities.

- Changes in the EC can help make the UK fairer and stronger, but only if this country contributes a positive vision of a stronger and fairer Europe.

# PREFACE

The Commission on Social Justice, established at the instigation of John Smith MP, Leader of the Labour Party, was launched fifty years after the publication of 'the Magna Carta of the welfare state' - the famous Beveridge Report *Social Insurance and Allied Services*. That document, and Beveridge's second report *Full Employment in a Free Society* in 1944, laid the basis for the 1945 Labour government's reforms of social security, employment, and health. That post-war 'settlement' endured for a generation.

Today, the future of welfare - including services like education and the NHS as well as financial benefits - is top of the political agenda. Although the social security budget totals nearly £80 billion, no one is satisfied. The Government is looking for ways to cut benefits and discourage claimants; but benefits are already so low that millions of children, parents and elderly people are going without basic necessities. If want and squalor were unacceptable fifty years ago, then they surely are today; but equally, it is true that because there are so many in need it is expensive to make benefits more generous. Benefit cuts or tax increases will only address the symptoms of economic failure - above all the £50 billion Public Sector Borrowing Requirement. The only way out of the impasse is to tackle the structural causes of poverty, and above all to extend opportunities for financial independence and personal security.

The sweeping changes proposed by Beveridge in 1942 came at an extraordinary historical moment. Amidst the unity of war, and after a terrible decade of economic depression and social division, he formulated a set of social and political ground rules for the post-war peace. His prescription for social solidarity, citizenship rights, and collective action embodied the national will for change. Today, no such consensus exists. While most people agree that we need change, there is confusion about what the changes should be.

The reality is that the country is caught in a vicious circle of economic underachievement and social polarisation. Welfare spending simply cannot keep pace with economic failure, and most obviously mass unemployment, low pay and poverty. But some of the strains on Britain's welfare state are shared in other parts of the industrialised world: there are fundamental changes affecting our economic and social life, and the comfortable assumptions of the post-war years - about employment, the position of women in society, and the role of the state - cannot be the basis of policy reform today.

We have to develop a new analysis for new and changing times. The purpose of this publication is to put the immediate debate in a longer term perspective, and set out in a preliminary way ideas about objectives and strategies to make this a fairer and stronger country, fit for the 21st century.

# 1
# INTRODUCTION

The welfare state that emerged from the extraordinary circumstances of the 1940s was the brain-child of John Maynard Keynes and William Beveridge. While Keynes seemed to have solved the problems of production, Beveridge calculated how to distribute the proceeds fairly. The intellectual authority of the political Right over the last twenty years has in large part come from the breakdown of this Keynesian and Beveridgean legacy. It is that breakdown, and the failure of the Thatcherite prescription successfully to replace it, that must be our starting point today.

In this section, we summarise Beveridge's three key assumptions and argue that they do not apply in today's world. In part 2, we propose four objectives to guide the development of policy. Part 3 looks to the future, and sets out the economic, social and political changes that will form the context in which our objectives must be realised. Finally, part 4 develops ten propositions about the strategies that might help us achieve our objectives.

## Beyond Beveridge

Fifty years ago, at the height of the Keynesian economic revolution, policy-makers assumed that through policies of national demand management the economy could guarantee employment for everyone seeking work. Today, in the grip of a global industrial revolution, national governments have to work within a macroeconomic framework increasingly determined by others. Failure of demand can of course cause a recession; but failure of supply - above all, lack of investment in skill, research, capital and infrastructure - is the cause of chronic economic weakness and long term underemployment. It is wrong to argue, as some do, that national governments are now merely passive victims of international economic forces, but the aims of policy have to change in order to build long term competitiveness and prosperity.

Next, Beveridge assumed fifty years ago that a woman's place was in the home of a two-parent family. 'By definition,' he wrote, 'the family is a group consisting of two parents, male and female respectively, and their offspring'. He asserted that 'In the next thirty years housewives as mothers have vital work to do in ensuring the adequate continuance of the British race and of British ideals in the world.'

Today, the situation is very different. Women make up nearly half the paid labour force and, in some regions, the majority. One child in five is being brought up by a lone parent, usually the mother. In the 1950s, full employment meant full-time, life-time work for men - 48 hours for 48 weeks for 48 years. Today, most women and a growing minority of men are employed part-time for part of their lives. A new balance has to be struck between family life and paid employment. Equal opportunities for women in the workplace - the usual focus of policy - demands new responsibilities from men in the home.

Finally, the welfare state of fifty years ago was built on the expertise of professionals. Too often, people were treated as passive recipients of services and benefits deemed appropriate by government. Today, partly as a result of the security and opportunity provided by the 1945 welfare state, but also because of its failures and limitations, people want to make more decisions for themselves.

The Commission must articulate these new realities. We want to express the unease that is increasingly felt at the failure of government to reflect them, and find new ways to develop the frustrated talents of the majority of citizens, who, even if they do not live in poverty, are not able to develop their talents to the full.

## A Radical Agenda

On the second page of his report in 1942, Beveridge set out three principles that should guide change. They concerned the radicalism and independence required of proposals for change.

Most famously, he said that proposals for the future should not be held back by the sectional interests of the present: 'A revolutionary moment in the world's history is a time for revolutions, not for patching' he wrote. Second, he insisted that want was only one of five giants on the road of reconstruction, the others being ignorance, disease, squalor and idleness: 'social insurance should be treated as one part only of a comprehensive policy of social progress', as he put it. Third, he emphasised the need for co-operation between the state and the individual.

These principles are as relevant now as they were in 1942. But today they must be applied not just to the failures of the last 14 years but also to the reform of the Beveridge model itself. We are not suffering, in Britain, a momentous war, but we are living in a time of momentous change. The vigour and rigour with which Beveridge attacked the obsolete inheritance of the years between the two World Wars exemplifies how we must treat what is obsolete in the system that we have inherited.

Above all, we must recognise that wealth and welfare go hand in hand, not only because wealth pays for welfare, but because social welfare - and above all, the opportunities provided by education and training, good health and a cohesive community - is a crucial factor in wealth creation. The central resource of a modern economy is the energy, talents and skills of its people.

In the 1940s, Beveridge needed Keynes. Today, a Commission on Social Justice which looks ahead to the 21st century must equally be a Commission on Economic Opportunity.

# 2
# OBJECTIVES FOR PUBLIC POLICY

Government intervention, economic or social, may have many different aims. In its 19th century forms, the welfare state was designed, among other things, to improve the fitness of soldiers (in France), and to undercut the appeal of socialist parties (in Germany under Bismarck). The extensive academic literature on the welfare state has ascribed to it the aims, among others, of mitigating poverty, increasing equity, reducing uncertainty, correcting market inefficiency, redistributing income over the life-cycle, and promoting social integration.

The Commission's first publication proposed a cumulative structure of ideas for thinking about justice and injustice in Britain today. We suggested there that the aims of social justice can best be understood in terms of four core ideas:

● **The foundation of a free society is the equal worth of all citizens.**

● **All citizens should be able as a right of citizenship to meet their basic needs for income, shelter, education, nutrition and health care.**

● **Self-respect and personal autonomy depend on the widest possible spread of opportunities and life-chances.**

● **Inequalities are not necessarily unjust but unjustified inequalities should be reduced and where possible eliminated.**

From this hierarchy of values, starting with the consensual notion of the equal worth of all citizens and proceeding to a radical conclusion concerning unjustified inequalities, we have derived four central objectives for government policy.

## The Objective of Security

Social justice, on any definition, demands the amelioration of poverty; but that is a second best. The aim should be to *prevent* poverty among families and individuals. 'Prevention where possible, relief where necessary' should be our guide.

## The Objective of Opportunity

Government policy should support and increase the autonomy and life-chances of every individual, whatever his or her birth or circumstance. What government can do *for* people is limited: but there are no limits to what people can be enabled to achieve for themselves.

## The Objective of Democracy

We need to diffuse power within government and to spread power from government to people in their regions, localities and communities. The more decisions people can make themselves, the better the decisions are likely to be.

## The Objective of Fairness

Not all inequalities are unfair. But where they are, they should be reduced and, if possible, eliminated. Our aim is to promote a fairer distribution of risks and rewards.

These goals do not by themselves tell us what public policy should be, but they do provide benchmarks by which the Commission - and the public - can judge policy options.

# 3
# THE THREE GREAT REVOLUTIONS

Social injustice in Britain today is shocking. Since 1979:

- the number of people in poverty (defined as those living on or below the income support level - currently less than £6000 per year for a family of four) has risen from 7.7 million to 11.3 million

- unemployment has tripled, and there are now two million men aged 16-64 not included in the unemployment figures but registered as 'economically inactive'

- tax cuts of £31.4 billion have given the top 1 per cent of income earners £33,300 per year, compared with £400 per year for the bottom *half* of earners; between 1979 and 1991, the income of the poorest 10 per cent of households fell by 14 per cent, and that of the top 10 per cent rose by over 50 per cent.

However, we must not be bewitched by 14 years of Conservative government. We need to look further back than the election of Mrs Thatcher in 1979, and further forward than an election in 1995, 1996 or even 1997. A diagnosis of injustice in Britain today, and prescriptions for improving the situation, call for a longer term (and more objective) view than one shaped by the constraints of the electoral cycle.

The post-war settlement in Britain, and in other industrialised countries, depended upon specific international conditions. These included the maintenance of free trade, including access to the USA's consumer and capital markets; the creation of a relatively open and stable international financial system agreed at Bretton Woods; the availability of secure and cheap Middle East oil supplies; and an end to war between the liberal capitalist states with the creation of NATO. In the last twenty years, however, the world has seen the breakdown of Bretton Woods; growing mobility and instability in world financial markets; the loss of control over oil supplies by the main Western consumers (Britain's North Sea Oil is a temporary windfall); the rapid industrialisation of the Pacific Rim; and of course the economic shocks of German unification and the collapse of the Communist economies of the Eastern bloc.

Thus, the international conditions for the post-war settlement have already been transformed. But so have the *national* conditions. The welfare states developed in Western Europe after the Second World War were founded on three interdependent pillars: full employment, the nuclear family, and the interventionist national state. In different countries, the relations between the three took different forms, the product of particular cultural, institutional and political variations. In Sweden, for example, an active labour market policy, highly egalitarian policies towards women, and universal public sector services combined to produce - until recently - a virtuous circle of low unemployment, high investment and extensive social provision. In Germany, by contrast, the economic miracle of the 1950s and 1960s was based on high wage, high skill employment for men, a traditional family structure, and a corporatist partnership between public and private sectors in the organisation of the economy.

In comparison with either of these countries, the UK was a hybrid. Our welfare institutions and practices were in part at the leading-edge of radical social reform, in part they lagged behind; in part they were collectivist, in part individualist; in part based on social citizenship, in part rooted in a contributory system; in part universal, in part means-tested. The list of anomalies could go on. The central point, however, is that the founding assumptions of the welfare state about each sphere - economic, social, and political - have to a greater or lesser extent been undermined. We now face three great revolutions:

- The economic revolution is a global revolution of skill, technology and competition that is transforming the nature and supply of work;

- The social revolution is a revolution of women's life-chances, of family structures and demography, but it is also a revolution of citizens' and consumers' expectations;

- The political revolution is a challenge to the assumptions of Parliamentary sovereignty and government power; it involves a fundamental reorientation of the relationship between those who govern and those who are governed.

These changes are partly the product of the welfare state itself, but they also reflect a range of other influences. They have profound implications for attempts to complete Beveridge's famous attack on the 'five great evils' of want, disease, ignorance, squalor and idleness, and also for the broader ambitions - to extend life-chances and limit unjustifiable inequalities - to which the Commission is committed.

## The Economic Revolution

At President-elect Clinton's 'economic summit' in Little Rock, Arkansas in December 1992, John Sculley, Chief Executive of Apple Computers, described a fundamental shift in the organisation of production and the nature of competition within market economies. The model of industrial production inaugurated by Frederick Taylor's scientific management and Henry Ford's mass production is now giving way to a new system, sometimes labelled 'lean production' or 'mass customisation', that combines the innovation and improvisation of craft production with the large-scale efficiencies of the industrial revolution.

These changes are being powered by the competitive edge of countries on the Pacific Rim, and they pose a fundamental challenge to industry and living standards in Europe. Capital, natural resources and - increasingly - people are available in global markets. We are all familiar with the threat posed to British textile workers' jobs by low-paid employees in the developing world. But international telecommunications and information technology make it possible to shift many other jobs around the globe. Swissair, for instance, has recently relocated its world-wide accounts operation to Bombay; the American giant General Electric is Singapore's biggest exporter.

John Sculley in his presentation to President Clinton's summit highlighted five features of the 'old economy': mass standardised production, mass consumption, centralised control of decision-making, high economies of scale for big domestic markets, and rigid standards and procedures laid down at the top. By contrast, in today's new model economy, goods must now be globally competitive and customised to individual demand. Decision making and quality control must be decentralised to the point of production, with goods transferred to the market quicker at lower cost. Echoing the main argument of the 1990 report from the Commission on the Skills of the American Workforce, *America's Choice*, Sculley summed up very simply the strategic choice facing policy makers: 'Do we want high skills, or low wages?'.

*High Skills or Low Wages?*

In Britain, the same choice has to be made. Between 1974/76 and 1986/88, the unemployment rate for workers with no qualifications rose from 2.5 to 4.6 times that of university graduates. Today, 44 per cent of the long term unemployed have no qualifications at all. Since 1982, the rate of income return to university education has risen by nearly half. At the same time we are a low cost and relatively low wage economy: our unit labour costs are now as low as those of Greece, Spain and Portugal, and job growth is mainly in low paid employment where employees have few employment rights. There are short term arguments about the attraction of these low costs to mobile capital; in the long term, they leave the UK less able to compete for high-skill, high-paid jobs, and intensely vulnerable to harsh competition from even lower-wage producers.

A Commission visit to Southampton Docks vividly illustrated the strategic choice facing Britain. At Southampton Container Terminals, dockers organised by the TGWU are negotiating with employers who are demanding a pay freeze and longer working hours and compulsory redundancies. In a situation reminiscent of the TIMEX dispute in Dundee, the union says that the employers are paying a new workforce of casual labour to remain on standby, ready to step in if the dockers go on strike.

A few hundred yards down the docks is Southampton Cargo Handling where TGWU members organised an employee buy-out from Associated British Ports. 'Every worker a shareholder' is the slogan on the company's literature, stressing that the worker/owners' commitment to quality and speed guarantees top-class service to customers. Gone are the old demarcations between white-collar and blue-collar workers: today, administrative staff drive vehicles onto waiting ships and nobody stops work until the loading is finished. Gone are the structures of 'us and them'; the motto today is 'us and us'. Honda, whose made-in-Britain cars are loaded by SCH, insists that the drivers wear white gloves while they are working. The image of dockers in white gloves sums up the possibility of competition based on quality and co-operation rather than cost-cutting and conflict.

To pay our way in world markets today, and preserve, let alone improve, our standard of living for tomorrow, UK companies need to compete in the market for quality goods and services by combining Savile Row service, Marks and Spencer quality and C&A prices. This is something we are not well placed to achieve: in John Sculley's terms, we are a 'resource poor' nation in the assets that matter in the new global marketplace.

The first of these resources is the skills of the workforce. David Sainsbury, the Chairman one of the UK's most successful businesses, said in a paper circulated to the Commission that it was this factor, and what he calls 'cumulative learning', that determines the standard of living of a country. As he put it:

> 'The world's best companies...are using the intelligence and skills of their workers more fully than in the past, and as a result are unleashing major advances in productivity, quality, variety and speed of new product introductions.'

Whether at the car manufacturer Rover, or in banks where tellers are being trained as all-round consultants, front-line workers are being given and taking personal responsibility for quality and innovation.

However, while governments in France as well as Korea and Japan are on course to have 80 per cent of young people reaching university entrance standard by the year 2000, the English, Welsh, Northern Irish, and to a lesser extent Scottish, education systems are designed to weed out all but the top one third by the age of 18,  At Nissan in Sunderland, where the Commission talked to employees, 7 out of ten job applicants fail to score 40 per cent on the company's verbal reasoning test. Meanwhile, among adults, the Adult Literacy and Basic Skills Unit reports that over 6 million people have problems with basic literacy and numeracy. Skill levels are 40 per cent below those of our neighbours, and two thirds of workers have no vocational or professional qualification at all.

Although Britain's universities provide world-class education in many subjects, the shortage of graduates in science, holds back our development: the number of students achieving at least two A levels (or three Scottish Highers) in science subjects halved from 29 per cent of school leavers in 1986 to 14 per cent in 1990 according to the CBI. Glaxo Pharmaceuticals, one of the UK's most successful companies, have pointed out that unless this trend is reversed, there will be a shortage of applicants for science courses at undergraduate level, with the inevitable result that British industry will suffer from a shortage of trained scientists and technicians. (There is already a shortage of graduate and post-doctoral organic chemists in the UK.)

## *Investment*

When it comes to investment, both public and private, in plant, equipment and infrastructure, the UK lags behind again. Britain invests about 18 per cent of national income each year, compared with 21 per cent in Germany and 27 per cent in Japan; newly industrialising countries like Korea and Singapore have been investing 35 per cent. Manufacturing investment has fallen by 25 per cent since 1990, and although Britain was top of the OECD countries in attracting inward investment during the 1980s, we were also top of the OECD league for *outward* investment, which was more than double the level of inward flows. Similarly, investment in research and development by UK industry is much lower than its international competitors, and has slipped further behind during the recession. A recent Department of Trade and Industry survey showed that UK companies devoted 1.55 per cent of aggregate sales revenue to R&D last year, compared with a world average of 4.59 per cent; as a share of profits, we invested only 19.7 per cent compared with a startling 94.3 per cent internationally.

Equally, in terms of public infrastructure, Britain's decaying transport system is a national embarrassment: trains coming through the channel tunnel from France will have to slow down once on the British mainland, from 190 to 100 miles per hour. It takes about an hour to reach central London by underground from Heathrow Airport, compared with 25 minutes to reach Charles de Gaulle airport in Paris from the Gare du Nord.

The UK economy therefore suffers from chronic underinvestment in both the public and the private sectors. Consumption as a share of national output has risen from around 60 per cent in the 1960s and 1970s to 65 per cent today. The result is a cycle of neglect not just on Easterhouse in Glasgow or Moss Side in Manchester or Newtown in Birmingham. Britain is the home base for many world-class companies and some world-class industries: but living standards in Britain as a whole have fallen behind those of Belgium, France and Northern Italy. We are now 18th out of the top 22 countries in the world league of national output. And according to the 1993 *World Competitiveness Report*, the UK's domestic economy rating is now 19th out of 22; Britain's manufacturing industry ranked bottom of the international league.

But there are other challenges to our social and economic institutions. For example, job creation can pose difficult challenges to those already in employment. Cutting unemployment without stimulating inflation requires new forms of pay-setting, as well as mechanisms to ensure that pay restraint is translated into jobs rather than increased profits. In a submission to the Commission, the Nobel prize-winning economist Professor James Meade argued that 'Keynesian full-employment policy ... collapsed simply and solely because a high level of money expenditures came to lead not to a high level of output and employment but to a high rate of inflation of money wages, costs and prices in spite of growing unemployment...It is very possible that to absorb two million extra workers into employment would require a considerable reduction in wage costs.'

Fritz Scharpf, one of Germany's leading political economists, has argued that full employment can only be recovered 'through a redistribution of existing work opportunities and working incomes at the expense of the great majority of those already employed.' The Commission will be examining what we mean by 'full employment' in the light of changing work and family patterns.

## Two Futures

The reality is that the UK faces two futures. In one, we continue to cut investment. Some companies and some people manage to do well, but unemployment stays high and the country as a whole falls further behind the rest of the European Community. We become locked ever more tightly into a 'low skills equilibrium' of low investment, low technology and low levels of education and training.

In the other future, we invest now for the sake of future prosperity. Unemployment falls, and the fear of unemployment is lifted from millions more. We make a concerted attempt to compete in the high value-added markets of high innovation, high technology, high skill and high investment.

In the first future, the average family will become less and less secure, squeezed between the decline in good jobs and the growing pressure for tax increases, public spending cuts or both. The poor - who became poorer still during the boom years of the 1980s - will become even poorer if low growth is our future, and insecurity and low wages will affect more and more people.

In the second future, living standards will also grow slowly for several years as we devote more of national output to investment. But economic growth will reduce if not eliminate the need for higher taxes; the quality of education, training and the other foundations of our economy will improve substantially; and falling unemployment will cut the numbers of people who depend on benefits, making it possible to maintain and even to increase the incomes of the poorest.

One is a low road which pits employers against employees in a struggle around shrinking competitiveness and cost-cutting; the other is a high road which offers the prospect of workers producing higher quality for their customers and getting higher rewards for themselves.

Neither future is easy, neither cheap. But only one offers any hope at all of social justice.

## The Social Revolution

A central theme of the work of the Commission is that economic policy is not separable from social policy: in fact, they are interdependent. Contrary to the guiding philosophy of the 1980s, we do not believe that the economy is an autonomous and self-regulating sphere that pays for necessary but burdensome social investment. There cannot be a healthy economy in a sickly society, because what goes on in society is vital for the nature and performance of the economy.

Richard Wilkinson's recent work, which establishes a strong correlation between relative income equality in a country and life expectancy is perhaps the most stark evidence for this. The relationship works the other way too: social inequality has an economic cost, in crime and unemployment for example.

The costs of social polarisation are acute. Poverty in the midst of plenty is not only morally unpleasant but also extremely expensive. It has been calculated that every high school dropout in the United States costs the country $300,000 over their lives in lost earnings, increased likelihood of crime and the like.

As we showed in our first publication, Britain remains a society scarred and held back by indefensible inequalities in opportunity, income, and power. Yet we are also a society which is changing fast. On none of the measures by which we describe our society - class, family, race, demography - are we the same society as we were fifty years ago. It is dangerous as well as easy to simplify, but along with the social changes that come about as men and women move slowly closer to equality in their opportunities and life-chances, other inherited assumptions are exposed to criticism, about rank for example, or religion, occupation, leisure, family and sexuality.

### Class

It has become conventional to hear people argue that class does not matter in Britain today; they say 'class is irrelevant'. We do not accept this; class still matters - it is still the most important determinant of a child's life chances.

At a secondary school in a reasonably well-off part of Birmingham, we asked 6th form students whether they thought Britain was a fair society. Only one thought it was. When we asked what they thought was unfair about Britain, class was the first thing they mentioned. Those students were right.

For example, the higher education system will soon cater for 1 million students, but entry remains highly stratified on class grounds. At the two extremes, only 1 per cent of women whose fathers are from social class V hold an undergraduate degree or equivalent, compared with 41 per cent of men with fathers from social class I. The sons and daughters of fathers in unskilled or semi-skilled jobs are one-third as likely to enter university as they would be if places were allocated at random.

However, it is the case that the class map of Britain, while still highly stratified, is changing. Manual workers formed over half the electorate twenty years ago, but only one third today. Fewer than 4 million people now work in manufacturing, once the heart of the industrial working class.

### Rich and Poor

Average living standards have, of course, increased massively since 1950. Then, the richest 10 per cent of families received one third of all income. For thirty years, the gap narrowed, steadily if slowly, so that by 1979, although the share of the top 10 per cent was still higher than that of the bottom half of all families, their share had fallen to just over a quarter of all income. (This fall was concentrated in the top 1 per cent, whose share fell from 11 per cent to just over 5 per cent.) Since 1979, this steady trend has gone into reverse; the gap has been widening again.

The structure of wealth and poverty have changed too. For example, whereas inheritance was the overwhelming source of wealth 50 years ago, fortunes made in retailing and production now appear regularly in the *Sunday Times* list of the 400 richest people in Britain.

Fifty years ago, Beveridge assumed that if someone was in work then they and their family were out of poverty. Conversely, if someone was out of paid work - because they were unemployed, sick or retired - then the whole family would be poor. It was on this basis that he established income benefits for those unemployed and retired. Today, his assumptions do not hold.

Unemployment remains one of the most important causes of poverty, but a growing proportion of the poor *earn* their poverty. Low wages in Britain today mean a security guard working a 12-hour shift for £1.20 - well below the levels prescribed by the Wages Councils which the Government is now abolishing. A care worker employed on low wages in a private nursing home in the West Lothian region of Scotland wrote to the Commission as follows:

> 'People are tired hearing that they have to accept low pay as a means of securing a *real* job. A real job to us means that you have enough to live on.'

For too many people, work simply doesn't pay. The result is that people are locked into benefit, and the country locked into its costs in terms of lost production as well as benefit payments. But while it is confusing and inefficient to tax someone into poverty, and then means-test them out of it, that is what the system too often does.

Equally, however, it is no longer the case that all those people not working are unable to support themselves. Fifty years ago, the vast majority of pensioners were poor, and so a benefit given to all pensioners on the basis of National Insurance Contributions could be an effective means of relieving poverty as well as encouraging savings. Today, however, pensioners show one of the widest distributions of income of any group in the population. For a growing number of retired people, the state pension is only part of a 'mixed economy' of pension provision.

## Race

Beveridge did not anticipate that Britain would become the multicultural, multiracial, multilingual and multifaith society that it is today. Public policy must come to terms with issues that it previously ignored. Today, for example, we need to root out the evil of racial discrimination, as well as the 'five great evils' identified by Beveridge.

White people with qualifications to A level standard or equivalent are 14 per cent more likely than Afro-Caribbeans who are as well qualified to get jobs in the top two occupational groups. Too often, black people bear a disproportionate share of economic hardship. For example, on the Commission's visit to Nottingham, we were told that while the unemployment rate was 19 per cent across the whole of the city, among Afro-Caribbean men aged 16-24 the figure is 41 per cent. In the late 1980s, women of Indian origin were two-thirds more likely to possess a degree qualification than the average for their sex - but were also two-thirds more likely to be unemployed.

At the same time, it is essential to recognise the complexities of the current picture, as the 'New Map of Injustice' in our first publication *The Justice Gap* tried to explain. For example, young Britons of Indian, African-Asian and Chinese origin are now achieving more in education and employment than their white counterparts.

## Families

Beveridge, like most policy-makers of his time, assumed that a woman's place was in the home. He built his social security system on the assumption that women were dependent on men, and that they would be provided for by them. In the last fifty years, however, the lives of increasing numbers of women, and hence of men, have been transformed by a range of forces: the automation of housework, the development of reproductive technology, rapidly growing levels of employment, the liberalisation of divorce laws, the equalisation of formal educational opportunity, and, along with these, radical changes in family structures. Today, fewer people are getting married, and more marriage is ending in divorce. Nearly half the British workforce are women, and the number is increasing. Yet change still has a long way to go - in employment, in the home, in politics - before the aspirations of many women are met. This has profound implications for public policy.

For example, the economic revolution at the workplace is also a fiscal revolution for government. What was previously done free by women - childcare and eldercare for example - is now in many cases being done by women in the employment of the state. As Jane Millar and Caroline Glendinning put it: 'women are service sector workers in and out of the family'. The demands made by the transformation in domestic relations are wide-ranging:

- for the government, a fundamental review of the bases of social security provision, child care and social services;

- for employers, new demands for flexible work patterns, support for childcare and other measures to accommodate caring work within the home;

- and for families, a renegotiation of the relationships between mothers, fathers and children.


## *Demography*

We are repeatedly told that we face a 'demographic timebomb' with growing numbers of elderly people dependent upon shrinking numbers of young workers. In fact, most of this increase has already taken place. The biggest increase in the numbers of elderly people actually occurred in the first half of this century. Nonetheless, the question of how we pay for our pensions, especially if more people continue to retire early, has to be faced. By detaching the basic retirement pension from earnings, and increasing it only in line with prices, the present Government has ensured - without any real public debate - that it will continue to lose value. But Jane Falkingham and Paul Johnson of the London School of Economics say that 'if the National Insurance pension is to maintain its current 15 per cent replacement rate, National Insurance contribution rates will need to rise by about seven percentage points by 2030 because of the rise in the ratio of pensioners to contributors'.

A potentially bigger issue arises regarding the health and community services on which many people, particularly the most elderly, depend. Retired people already do much productive (often caring) work outside the paid economy, but as the number of elderly people in our population grows, so the question of who does the caring will become more acute. In 1900, for every person aged over 85 there were 24 women in their

50s. By 2000, the ratio will be 3 to 1 - and most of those women in their 50s will also be in paid employment. We cannot and should not continue to assume that women, rather than men, will take on most unpaid caring work, and that this social care is a purely private responsibility.

## The Political Revolution

Economic and social reform must be supported in the political sphere. It is politics - political coalitions, popular attitudes, institutional structures - that makes possible or blocks proposals for change. The 1990s are, however, a time of particular political openness.

The collapse of the commanding ideologies of the 20th century - soviet communism, Keynesian social democracy, Thatcherite neo-liberalism - has left a political vacuum. The communist experiment, far from resolving the inefficiency and waste involved in free market capitalism, fuelled both. Keynesian social democracy promised to smooth the business cycle, and for thirty years after the Second World War did so, but in an interdependent world economy found its prescription less and less reliable; Keynes had not solved the problem of production after all. Finally, the received economic answer to the limitations of the 1945 settlement, a return to *laissez-faire* economics of the minimal state and free markets, has in turn produced a cycle of debt, recession and social polarisation in the countries where it has been most vigorously pursued.

The 1990s are a time of political uncertainty rather than national unity. Since old ideas do not work, it is a good time to develop new ones; or as the American economist Peter Drucker puts it, 'This is the time to *make the future* - precisely because everything is in flux'. At Handsworth College in Birmingham, the Principal, Chris Webb, summed up the Commission's task when he said: 'We need to invent a national mission - we need to invent a future'.

### Reinventing Government

The challenge to politics and government is defined by the growing and changing demands on it and the growing constraints on what it can achieve. David Osborne, co-author of the American bestseller *Reinventing Government* identifies four factors that explain the pressures on public services across the industrialised world: the pace of social and technological change, and the difficulties this poses for traditional, top-down government bureaucracies; the expectations of the public, for quality and choice; the impact of the global marketplace, and the need to attract mobile capital; and finally, the sheer expense of government. To these should be added the growing demand from women, ethnic minorities and disabled people for a political system which better reflects their concerns and demands.

On the 'demand' side, pressure is exerted by demographic forces, by technical innovation and by medical advance. It has been estimated for example that spending on personal social services needs to grow by 2.5 per cent per annum rate to keep pace with demand, and that the NHS must grow by 2 per cent per annum in real terms if it is to keep pace with increasing medical technology and costs. On the supply side, the constraints on government spending come from such sources as the electorate's scepticism about increased taxation, international pressure for a convergence of tax levels, and conflicts between generations over the distribution of resources.

In addition, public services suffer from a 'relative price effect'. Although doctors, nurses and other staff in the NHS, for instance, have recently achieved substantial increases in productivity, it generally remains the case that it is more difficult to achieve, and to measure, rising productivity in services than in manufacturing. Service sector activities like teaching children or helping elderly people look after themselves, necessarily involve a high input of labour. Because wages rise fairly consistently across the economy, then the faster we increase productivity in the trading sector to meet world competition, the faster the relative costs of services grow. The challenge is to meet increasing demand at manageable cost.

## *Political Leadership*

However, just when imaginative political and civic leadership is most needed, people feel great distrust in the designs - grand or otherwise - of politicians. As one councillor put it to the Commission in Newcastle:

> 'The issue on the doorstep is not "why should I vote Labour",
> but "why should I vote at all?"'.

This is in part a legacy of the 1980s, when the dominant ideology was that economic and social decline were the product of government intervention, and that markets, and not politics, held the solution to our problems. However, the decline of faith in politics itself goes deeper: the claims and actions of politicians seem increasingly distant from the decisions of the people who vote for them.

It is important to see that the welfare state which developed after 1945 has been undermined politically as well as economically and socially, above all because it failed to make citizens feel it was theirs. The exception of the National Health Service almost proves the rule. One reason for the political failures is that the 1945 consensus was directed to the *national* state, but the national level is increasingly too small for the big problems, and too big for the small problems. There is pressure for decentralisation of some decision-making to local government and other issues move to Europe. It is in any case more and more difficult to forge effective national policies through national institutions when the complexity and speed of change of modern societies makes it more and more difficult to govern society from the top-down.

The Fabian conception was one in which people were profoundly dependent on government. Individual problems were to be solved by experts, and there were few, if any mechanisms for ordinary people to participate in decisions affecting their own lives. Perhaps the paradigm case is the treatment of disabled people: the concept of 'need' has been and must be central to social justice, but its definition has been dominated by professionals, too often to the exclusion of disabled people themselves.

There was in various public service activities a powerful ethos of 'government knows best', illustrated by the infamous story of the council tenants who were refused permission to paint their front door the colour they wanted. A new course for public policy must be grounded not in paternalism but in participation and democracy.

There is, however, a final paradox in the current debate about the renewal of social policy. Everyone agrees that £80 billion of expenditure is not halting the increase in poverty and social division; few people believe that anyone actually likes paying taxes; yet the polls suggest that substantial, and more significantly increasing majorities in the population say they are in favour of greater spending on social welfare. British Social Attitudes surveys report that the number of people supporting an increase in taxation to provide better public services doubled between 1983 and 1991. In a 'Breadline Britain' survey for London Weekend Television, 25 per cent of people in 1983 were willing to pay an extra 5p in the pound in tax to help everyone afford items agreed to be necessities, while 59 per cent rejected the idea; by 1991, 44 per cent supported the idea and 44 per cent were still against it.

Greater personal independence, paradoxically, means increasing social interdependence. Whether the issue is environmental protection, teamwork in the workplace, or the promotion of safety in local communities, we are more and more dependent on others for what we are able to do alone. The challenge to the Commission is to develop new mechanisms of collective action which will at the same time meet common goals and liberate individual talent.

# 4
## TEN PROPOSITIONS ON SOCIAL JUSTICE

Faced with this rapidly changing economic, social and political world, the Commission has in the course of its first six months' work developed some preliminary impressions and ideas about how the values and objectives set out in Part 2 might be realised. The Commission will over the next six to eight months be testing these and other ideas, as well as developing detailed policy proposals. The ideas are presented here in the form of ten propositions about social justice and how it can be furthered in the UK. The propositions have been developed to stimulate debate, and represent preliminary thoughts.

### Proposition 1

**Social justice is about more than poverty - it concerns everyone. The best way to help the minority who are poor is to advance social justice for all.**

The Commission on Social Justice is not only a commission on social security or a commission on poverty. We are sceptical, on grounds of sociological fact and political efficacy, of the notion of a 'one third-two thirds' society, in which the 'contentment' of the top two thirds precludes help for the poorest. First, society is divided on grounds of race and gender as well as income. Further, not only are the aspirations of the bottom third - for financial security and economic opportunity - similar to those of the population as a whole, but the middle third at least has the same fears as those on lower income - about the insecurity of employment, the schooling offered their children, and the risk of crime.

Contrary to the 'trickle-down' theory of the 1980s, making the rich richer does not make the poor richer too. Indeed, because the great majority pay the costs of unemployment, crime and ill-health, making the poor poorer makes us all poorer too. Common interests demand social cohesion rather than polarisation.

### Proposition 2

**Paid work for a fair wage is the most secure and sustainable way out of poverty and it must be a goal of policy to extend the employment to those currently without it. A new commitment to full employment also requires a new approach to the distribution of paid and unpaid work. The tax-benefit system must create incentives for paid employment and help meet the needs of those performing unpaid work. Discrimination is an evil to be ranked alongside Beveridge's 'five great evils', and must be attacked whatever its form.**

Full employment was a basic assumption of the 1945 welfare state. Today, we cannot assume it. But full employment must become a central objective of policy again to enable people to enjoy real independence, and to provide the services on which we all at various stages in our lives depend. There is no shortage of work to be done: the issue instead is how we distribute paid and unpaid work between men and women, and across people's own lifecycles.

We believe that work - unpaid as well as paid - has a value for individuals itself. For proof of the value of a job, one only has to ask someone who has not got one; for evidence of the dignity offered by voluntary activity, one only has to ask the volunteers at the St Peter's Centre in Birmingham, who told us that they were proud to tell their friends that they worked at the Centre. 'Work is part of welfare, not its antithesis', as Howard Glennerster puts it.

Full employment today cannot mean, as it meant forty years ago, full-time work for men. The majority of women, and a growing minority of men, work part-week or part-year for at least part of their lives. For millions of people with young children, or nearing retirement, or wanting to combine employment with further education, part-time employment is a positive choice. But most part-time employees still lack the employment and social security rights of full-time employees, pro rata pay and the protection of public or private pension schemes.

The demands of economic competitiveness mean that flexible employment is here to stay for men and women, and the challenge for policy is to make it work for all individuals over their life-cycle. Paid work today must allow men and women to balance their responsibilities to career and family.

The Commission will be examining all forms of discrimination, and how they can be overcome. The potential as well as needs of disabled people is too often ignored by politicians as well as employers; Britain's ethnic minorities often face discrimination in the search for employment; and women still suffer from a pay gap in comparison to men.

### Proposition 3

**The tax-benefit system must serve a number of objectives. It is an important means by which we fulfil our obligations to each other, and by which we insure ourselves against unemployment, ill-health, and old age. Overall, those who can afford to contribute most should do so, and those who need most should receive it. Redistribution of income is a means to social justice and not an end in itself; social justice demands sufficient revenue to meet basic needs and extend opportunities, but there are limits of principle as well as practice to levels of taxation.**

Most of the present debate about 'targeting' versus 'universality' is based on a flawed understanding of the tax and benefits system. In particular, commentators - and Government Ministers - too often treat benefits separately from tax reliefs. For instance, those who object to child benefit for all mothers almost never object to personal tax allowances for all taxpayers or mortgage tax relief for all home-buyers. From the individual's point of view, receiving benefit and receiving a tax allowance may be very different; from the point of view of the Treasury, the two systems have exactly the same effect on public finances.

The Commission starts from the basic principle that the financial relationship between citizen and state encompasses, equally, the payment of taxes and the receipt of benefits and services. In all its aspects, the relationship should be fair, comprehensible and efficient. The present tax and benefit system in the UK meets none of these criteria; it badly needs an overhaul. For instance, it is plagued by benefit 'traps' that keep people in poverty, and despite the abolition of the most regressive tax of all, the poll tax, it remains the case that the richest 10 per cent of households pay 32 per cent of their income in tax, while the bottom 10 per cent pay 43 per cent of their income in tax. In other words, poverty in the UK is partly tax-induced.

Recent work has shown the extent to which the welfare state - including education and the NHS as well as financial benefits - acts as a lifetime 'savings bank'. Redistribution across the life-cycle is more significant than redistribution between different individuals. On average, well over half of the benefits and services people receive have been paid for by their own contributions. The tax-benefit system must continue to serve multiple objectives: those for whom paid work is either not possible or appropriate should be guaranteed sufficient to enable them to meet their basic needs and enjoy personal autonomy, and the tax-benefit system will continue to act as a lifetime 'savings bank' for benefits and services.

We already live in a 'mixed economy' of welfare, where private pensions and other forms of savings are increasingly important in ensuring individuals' security. Assumptions about 'public bad, private good' - or vice versa - are a wholly inadequate guide to policy. Instead, we need to be clear about our objectives, and then to find the fairest and most efficient way of meeting them.

The principles of social justice provide a clear and compelling basis for taxation (including but not limited to the taxation of incomes) to ensure that basic needs are met and opportunities extended. But that does not mean that principles of social justice recognise no limits to taxation. Principles cannot tell us precisely what the limits of taxation should be, but punitive levels are not justifiable. In addition, there are practical reasons - particularly within an increasingly integrated European Community - why Britain cannot afford levels of personal taxation above those of Germany, France and our other partners.

## Proposition 4

**At a time of rapid social and economic change, the most profound advantage is the ability to cope with change; public policy should be designed to extend this capability across the population.**

We live in a time of rapidly growing personal insecurity - in employment, in local communities, in families. The distribution of risk - of unemployment, crime, abuse - is a major political issue, and establishes new lines of political division. Security does not come by shielding people from change, by clinging to old jobs for example, and resisting the need for new skills and retraining. Nor does it come from simply promising a safety-net if things go wrong. As Katherine Duffy of the EC's Poverty 3 programme told the Commission: 'Unemployment is not about why you lost your last job, but why you don't get a new one'.

Forty years ago, a young man starting a job could confidently expect to stay in the same line of business or even in the same company until he retired. Security meant insurance against illness or unemployment, and provision for retirement. Today, the average man or woman can expect to change jobs between five and ten times. Millions of people will do so even more often. But every time old skills become redundant, every time a job change is required, there is a danger of the individual slipping down into less secure employment - or, like the men made redundant from industry in their 40's and 50's today, never getting employment again.

In a just society, collective endeavour will shape change for the benefit of the majority. Today, the essence of security is the ability to cope with change, to learn new skills and to find new opportunities. Thus, what we demand from schools in a changing world is not simply that children acquire specific skills and information, but that they also learn how to learn, how to become confident in their own ability to meet new challenges. But the implications go well beyond schools : as people change jobs more frequently, education and retraining will need to become a regular part of working life.

## Proposition 5

### Social justice demands a widening of access to wealth.

The policy which still sums up the appeal of Thatcherism for millions of working-class families is the right to buy one's council home. Although home ownership has produced nightmares of negative equity and repossession for some people, it remains central to the lives and aspirations of the majority of British people. We will, of course, be looking at the policies needed to ensure that everyone can afford a decent home, whether rented or bought. Here, we are concerned with the financial independence which home ownership can offer.

Home ownership is by no means the only way of creating a fairer distribution of wealth. About two-thirds of employed men and just over half of employed women contribute to occupational pension schemes, which between them have some £482 billion in assets including over 30 per cent of all UK-listed securities. Some 4 million people have also taken out personal pensions. But pension fund members do not, in any real sense, 'own' their pension funds. As the Maxwell scandal showed, pension fund regulation is grossly inadequate. Even when the fund is impeccably managed, the vast majority of contributors, because they leave the fund before retirement, do not gain anything like the value of the contributions which they and their employers have made. Personal pensions, with their high administrative costs, may represent even worse value for contributors - although they are, unlike occupational pensions, fully transferable between different jobs. The Commission will be looking at ways of giving pension fund contributors real ownership of what could be a substantial asset for individuals. Similarly, we will be looking at ways to develop democratic employee share ownership plans which can offer people a say in the decisions of their company, as well as a stake in its profits.

## Proposition 6

**The British economy requires a major shift from short term consumption towards long term investment in people, ideas and infrastructure. Public investment must become a catalyst for wealth creation.**

The British economy has been notable for many years for the wild swings between the bullish years of growth and the bearish years of slump. This instability is in itself bad for the economy, but underlying it is a fundamental failure of investment - above all in people and their education and (re)training, but also in infrastructure. This has to change if sustainable economic growth is to be achieved. It requires a new settlement between all who hold a stake in the success of a company - not just its shareholders, but its workers, bankers, and suppliers.

The present recession is the price we are all paying for the excess consumption of the 1980s. But the corollary is uncomfortable: if we are to return the British economy to an acceptable level of investment, personal consumption for several years will have to grow considerably more slowly than the economy as a whole. That means hard choices for government as well as individuals. The more we invest in education and training in the short term, for example, the less there will be available for tax cuts or benefit increases. If investment is given the priority we believe it deserves, the poorest must also be protected at least against any further fall in their living standards; indeed, they need and should have a real increase in their incomes. In other words, we have to make the cake bigger as well as share it out more fairly.

There are considerable savings to be made within the government budget, as well as ways of improving tax efficiency, and we will be examining them in detail. But there is a growing debate about a structural mismatch between government income and expenditure, the narrowing of the tax base in the 1980s, and the need to increase taxation: we will be making our own judgment about what is needed, and how taxation can be reformed to make it fairer and more efficient, as well as more acceptable.

## Proposition 7

**A strong community must support its families; we cannot expect families to shore up weak communities. Strong families come in different forms, but they are founded on stable and committed parenting. Children are '100 per cent of our future', and family policy should seek to give them the best start in life.**

We have discussed in this publication the changing shape of families in Britain - for example the rise in divorce, single parenthood, cohabitation and lesbian and gay relationships. Policy must work with the grain of social change, but it must at the same time be founded on clear principles - that children have a right to be dependent, that strong families require strong and independent women, and fathers need to accept emotional as well as financial responsibility for their children. The life-chances of children - the group Sylvia Hewlett powerfully calls '100 per cent of our future' - are a central concern of the Commission, and high on our list of priorities will be their need and society's need for the commitment of time, money and care from their parents and the wider community.

## Proposition 8

**Social cohesion has economic value in itself, and strong communities are the bedrock of economic regeneration. In Britain, these communities are neglected by a concentration of power at Westminster to the detriment of legitimate demands for increased power from the nations, regions and localities of Britain.**

In visits around the country, the Commission has seen how much is achieved by community and voluntary organisations, sometimes in partnership with the local authority, sometimes independent of it. The role of the public sector should be as much to catalyse and support these initiatives as it is to replace them; they are a key route to community regeneration. Public and private sectors are now interdependent: the conventional opposition of market to state is unhelpful. Today's debate must be about the values that govern the partnership between public and private, and the most effective combinations of the two.

In the Commission's visits around the country we have seen areas blighted by economic waste - in cities but also outside them - blessed with strong and vibrant communities, often led by women. The social cohesion of the people we have met is itself a potential source of economic strength, and economic development must build on this strength. It is what Robert Putnam calls the stock of 'social capital', embodied in trust, norms and networks built up over generations.

Strong communities are a foundation for individual development, but they are also good in themselves. The evidence from Europe, for example, is that economic growth must be stimulated not simply through macroeconomic reform, but through microeconomic change from the ground up that is based on the skills and resources of the local community. As Putnam puts it: 'social capital is not a substitute for effective public policy but rather is a prerequisite for it, and in part a consequence of it.'

Our political system is, however, now the most centralised in Europe, and almost seems designed to frustrate local initiative. In the context of growing social interdependence, the state in its relations with individuals and communities must be concerned to promote personal and community independence.

### Proposition 9

**While the welfare state has been founded on rights, society cannot work without parallel responsibilities and obligations. To strengthen rights, as we must, involves heightened responsibilities.**

In his famous schema of social change over three centuries - the development of civil rights in the 18th century, political rights in the 19th, and fully-fledged social citizenship in the 20th - the British sociologist T.H. Marshall focused on the slow accumulation of rights to representation, the vote, housing and education of the mass of ordinary people. What he did not develop were the parallel responsibilities that are an inevitable part of the development of rights. A strong sense of entitlement has been central to social progress over the centuries; unless it is accompanied by a strong sense of obligation, service or participation, we will not build the social bonds necessary for a just society.

The policy ramifications of this commitment are wide-ranging. For example, men who father children should take on a responsibility to help support them. While the details of the recent Child Support Act leave a lot to be desired - the legislation has been driven more by a Treasury desire to save money than the social need to promote responsible fatherhood - the principle of paternal responsibility should be upheld. Similarly, there is a balance between rights and responsibilities at the workplace. When employers can sack and lock out employees almost at will, the balance between the 'right to manage' and the responsibility to employees and the community has clearly gone wrong.

Further, because we are a society, the right to the rewards of one's effort is balanced by a responsibility to put something back - financially through taxes, personally through public service - into the community on which our personal success rests. Finally, we all have a collective responsibility not just to each other but to future generations. The right to use the resources of the planet is balanced by the responsibility that we hand it on to future generations in as good a state as that in which we found it.

## Proposition 10

**Britain has a distinctive contribution to make to the development of the European Community, but it also has things to learn and gain. Social and economic policy should not simply aim to establish minimal compatibility with European practice, but instead contribute a positive vision of a strong and fair community.**

Increased European integration - economic, political, and cultural - is inevitable and desirable, but the shape and structure of this integration remains to be established. In other words, the EC needs a new political project to complement the economic one that has taken it forward for forty years.

The EC has already begun to grasp the need for co-ordinated policies for growth and employment. We share the concern of many, however, that if the implementation of the Maastricht Treaty takes on a deflationary bias, it would undermine the effectiveness of such policies.

Britain must indeed be at the heart of Europe, but that requires a wholehearted engagement with the development of the EC as a social and political community, and not just an economic one. Issues of political organisation, defence and security fall well beyond our ambit, but we will be looking at how the development of the EC in the economic and social sphere can help Britain's development as a stronger and fairer country, and help Britain contribute to a more just distribution of resources between countries. A strong British contribution to the debate about European integration is important for Britain and Europe.

# 5
## CONCLUSION

The ten propositions on social justice conclude this discussion document, the second issued by the Commission as the basis for further debate and deliberation. In this publication we have covered a large number of issues that fall within the Commission's remit, and also left some out. Ours is a wide-ranging and ambitious project. We have moved from a set of values detailed in our first discussion document to establish four preliminary objectives for the Commission's work, and to set out our understanding of the context in which these objectives must be realised.

All the evidence suggests that there are no quick fixes, no easy answers, to Britain's problems. But throughout our discussions we have been encouraged and sometimes inspired by the talent and energy and innovation that we have seen in our visits around the country. These resources are the only basis on which one can hope to achieve change, and it is from the evidence of our visits that we have drawn up the ten propositions outlined in part 4 of this report.

The purpose of the ten propositions is partly to clarify for ourselves the key issues that we must tackle, but also to stimulate reaction and comment from organisations and individuals around the country. There is already great interest in the Commission's work - from businesses and trade unions, community groups and local authorities, academics and the general public - and it is from these sources of expertise and experience that the Commission draws its strength. In the autumn of 1993 and winter of 1993/4, we will be publishing a series of further discussion papers to take forward the debate. If this report can help harness the energy and ideas of the many people who want to contribute to our work, then it will have played an important part in the Commission's longer term aim, to help sow the seeds for a new and radical consensus for change in Britain.

## SOURCES AND FURTHER READING

**Beveridge W** (1942) *Social Insurance and Allied Services* (London: HMSO).

---------------- (1944) *Full Employment in a Free Society* (London: HMSO).

**Confederation of British Industry** (1992) *Making it in Britain* (London)

**Deacon A** (1991) *Rereading Titmuss: Morality, Work and Welfare* (Inaugural Lecture, University of Leeds).

**Drucker P** (1993) *Post-Capitalist Society* (Oxford: Butterworth-Heinemann).

**Esping-Andersen G** (1990) *The Three Worlds of Welfare Capitalism* (Princeton, New Jersey: Princeton University Press).

**International Institute for Management Development** (1993) *The World Competitiveness Report 1993* (Lausanne).

**Evans M and Glennerster H** (1993) *Squaring the Circle? The Inconsistencies and Constraints of Beveridge's Plan* (London: LSE Welfare State Programme).

**Falkingham J and Johnson P** (1993) *A Unified Funded Pension Scheme for Britain* (London: LSE Welfare State Programme).

**Falkingham J et al** (1993) *William Beveridge versus Robin Hood: Social Security and Redistribution over the Life-Cycle* (London: LSE Welfare State Programme).

**Field F** (1992) 'Durham Lectures' (February).

**Galbraith J K** (1992) *The Culture of Contentment* (London: Sinclair-Stevenson).

**Glennerster H** (1992) *Paying for Welfare* (London: Harvester Wheatsheaf).

**Goldblatt D** 'Britain in the International Political Economy: Implications for Social Justice' (Submission to the Commission).

**Hewlett S A** (1991) *When the Bough Breaks* (New York: Basic Books).

**Hills J**    (1988) *Changing Tax* (London: CPAG).

---------- (ed) (1990) *The State of Welfare* (Oxford: Clarendon Press).

**Jordan B *et al*** (1992) *Trapped in Poverty: Labour Market Decisions in Low Income Households* (London: Routledge).

**Keegan V** (1992) *The Spectre of Capitalism* (London: Radius).

**London Weekend Television** (1991) *Breadline Britain* 1990 (London).

**Marshall T H** (1992) *Citizenship and Social Class* (London: Pluto Press).

**Meade J** '14 Propositions on Social Justice' (Submission to the Commission).

**Millar J and Glendinning C** (1992) *Women and Poverty in Britain* (London: Harvester Wheatsheaf).

**Monk S** (ed) (1992) *From the Margins to the Mainstream* (London: National Council for One Parent Families).

**National Centre on Education and the Economy**(1988) *America's Choice: high skills or low wages!* (New York).

**National Institute for Social Work** (1992) *Who Owns Welfare?*

**Oppenheim C** (1993) *Poverty: The Facts* (London: CPAG).

**Osborne D and Gaebler T** (1992) *Reinventing Government* (New York: Addison-Wesley).

**Putnam R** (1993) 'The Prosperous Community: Social Capital and Public Life' in *The American Prospect* Number 13.

**Reich R** (1991) *The Work of Nations* (London: Simon and Schuster).

**Sainsbury D** 'Company Performance and Employee Participation' (Submission to the Commission).

**Scharpf F** (1991) *Crisis and Choice in European Social Democracy* (New York: Cornell University Press).

**Snower D** (1993) *The Future of the Welfare State* (London: CEPR).

**Walker R** (1991) *Thinking About Workfare* (London: SPRU/HMSO).

**Wilkinson R** (1992) 'Income distribution and life expectancy' in *British Medical Journal* 1992.

**Womack J** *et al* (1991) *The Machine that Changed the World: The Story of Lean Production* (New York: Harper Perennial).

# THE COMMISSION ON SOCIAL JUSTICE
## Terms of Reference

The Commission on Social Justice was set up with the following terms of reference:

- To consider the principles of social justice and their application to the economic well-being of individuals and the community;

- To examine the relationship between social justice and other goals, including economic competitiveness and prosperity;

- To probe the changes in social and economic life over the last fifty years, and the failure of public policy to reflect them adequately; and to survey the changes that are likely in the foreseeable future, and the demands they will place on government;

- To analyse public policies, particularly in the fields of employment, taxation and social welfare, which could enable every individual to live free from want and to enjoy the fullest possible social and economic opportunities;

- And to examine the contribution which such policies could make to the creation of a fairer and more just society.

## Membership

The 16 members of the Commission on Social Justice are:

| | |
|---|---|
| **Sir Gordon Borrie (Chairman)** | Former Director-General of Fair Trading |
| **Professor A B Atkinson, FBA** | Professor of Political Economy, University of Cambridge. |
| **Anita Bhalla** | Treasurer, Asian Resource Centre, Birmingham. |
| **Professor John Gennard** | Professor of Industrial Relations, University of Strathclyde. |
| **Very Rev John Gladwin** | Provost, Sheffield Cathedral. |
| **Christopher Haskins** | Chief Executive, Northern Foods, PLC. |
| **Patricia Hewitt** | Deputy Director, IPPR. |
| **Dr Penelope Leach** | President, Child Development Society. |
| **Professor Ruth Lister** | Professor and Head of the Deptartment of Applied Social Studies, University of Bradford. |
| **Emma MacLennan** | Vice Chair, Low Pay Unit. |
| **Professor David Marquand** | Professor of Politics, University of Sheffield. |
| **Bert Massie** | Director, Royal Association for Disability and Rehabilitation. |
| **Dr Eithne McLaughlin** | Lecturer in Social Policy, Queen's University of Belfast. |
| **Steven Webb** | Economist, Institute for Fiscal Studies. |
| **Margaret Wheeler** | Director of Organisation Development, UNISON. |
| **Professor Bernard Williams** | White's Professor of Moral Philosophy, University of Oxford. |

## Evidence

The Commission has already received a large number of informal submissions from individuals and organisations about our remit, the problems we must confront, and the strategies we should adopt to solve them. We also know, however, that many people want to submit formal evidence to the Commission, covering their ideas for social reform, economic renewal and political change.

With the publication of our first two discussion documents, of which this is the second, the Commission has completed the first phase of its work - a preliminary ground-clearing and objective-setting exercise. We are now entering phase 2, when we will be looking in some detail at various policy options, and how they can help us realise the objectives set out in this publication. We will over the course of the second half of 1993 and the beginning of 1994 be publishing a series of shorter discussion papers about certain aspects of public policy, and they may provoke further thinking.

We would therefore very much welcome written evidence from any quarter. Oral hearings may be held, but none are yet planned.

Anyone wishing to contact the Commission can do so through either its London or Glasgow office, at the following addresses:

**Commission on Social Justice**
**Institute for Public Policy Research**
**30-32 Southampton Street**
**London WC2E 7RA**
**(tel: 071 379-9400)**


**Commission on Social Justice**
**c/o Centre for Housing Research**
**Glasgow University**
**25 Bute Gardens**
**Glasgow G12 8RT**
**(tel: 041 339-8855 ext.4675)**